Spiritual Guidance through Godly Counselling

Merica Cox

2011

Spiritual Guidance through Godly Counselling

First Edition February 2011
ISBN 978-0-9565358-4-9
© Merica Cox 2009-2011

Merica Cox has asserted her rights under the Copyright, Designs and Patents act 1988 to be identified as the author of this work.

All rights reserved in all media. This book may not be copied, stored, transmitted or reproduced in any format or medium without specific prior permission from the author.

Published by:
CGW Publishing
B 1502
PO Box 15113
Birmingham
B2 2NJ
for
Balm of Gilead World Ministries
www.bogministries.org
info@bogministries.org

Reviews for Spiritual Guidance through Godly Counselling

The lack of good Godly counsel is prevalent in the church of Jesus Christ today. Many people are using counselling systems which are based in worldliness and ungodliness, using technical jargon and psychology thought up by people who themselves seem to have needed help with their own frame of mind.

Mrs Merica Cox has sought to remedy some of this, by writing what I consider to be a very bible-based book on counselling. Her central theme is one of scripturally inspired compassion for the counsellee. Her search for concern for the person needing good scriptural guidance through the malaise of their life can be summed up in one word – "LOVE". Jesus Christ was Love Personified and so Mrs Cox has sought to counsel using the same tactics that He and the best of His servants would use. The Apostle Paul said in one of the most famous sections of inspired writing, "Love never fails". Using the principles explained cannot possibly fail because they are all based in the love of God.

This work challenges us to make sure we have proper motivation in seeking to help others. That we are not doing it in order to make a name for ourselves, or for monetary gain, but to see people set free and, as a result, see the Kingdom of God increase.

There are many good books on counselling, and this one can be used in conjunction with them because it will help to ensure that the counsellor has a good relationship with the Lord and is truly seeking to fulfil His will.

Pastor Lindsey Mann

Lindsey has been a minister for over thirty years. He has travelled extensively to many countries with especial emphasis on Mauritius, Nigeria and Mexico. He has helped to pioneer a bible school in Africa and is currently on the faculty of a number of bible schools in London. Lindsey was a local Pastor for the Elim Pentecostal Churches for 15 years before entering into an itinerant ministry. In 1988 he experienced a visitation from the Lord in which he discovered that "God is nice, and He likes me!" Lindsey is ordained with New Life Ministries of Austin, Indiana under the auspices of Pastor Jeremy Hilderbrand. He has a Master's degree in Religious Education.

Dedication

This book has been dedicated to those who have suffered through inappropriate counselling or ministry. It is also dedicated to those who will need counselling in the future and to those who wish to become good counsellors.

I was motivated by the mistakes I made and those I saw in the body of Christ due to well meaning zealous people who without knowledge or understanding tried to minister, give direction and guidance to others.

I was particularly concerned by the number of people in the Christian community who took away their own lives. I questioned where we as the church failed them in their hour of need.

There is no price for a human soul; Jesus paid with his own blood, and we show great respect and care for people and for the word of God.

The bible says not many should teach but rather listen and learn for there will be greater judgement to those who teach others.

Contents

Reviews for Spiritual Guidance through Godly Counselling 3

Dedication 5

Preface 8

Introduction 13

Satellite Navigation as a Picture of Spiritual Guidance 23

What is Counselling? 28

    Case Study 31

Using the Word in counselling 38

Dealing with guilt 50

Dealing with Negativity 54

Counselling Techniques 57

    What type of questions to ask 59

    Fear and anger 63

    Discouragement and hopelessness 68

The Counselling Session 74

Stages of Counselling..................................77
    Relationship..77
    Recognition...77
    Identify solutions......................................78
    Action plan..78
    Family dynamics..79
Being Counselled..84
Counselling and the Deliverance Ministry.....88
Conclusion..99
Protecting Your Greatest Asset:
Your Mind...102
The Balm of Gilead World Ministries..........104

Preface

Mark 6:34, *"And Jesus, when he came out, saw many people, and was moved with compassion towards them, because they were as sheep not having a shepherd: and he began to teach them many things."*

The heart of God has always been for the welfare of his people. For God so loved the world and its people that he gave his only begotten son so that whosoever believes in him should not perish but have everlasting life.

God gave his people the Bible which is his word so that they could be guided in everything they do while in this world. The Bible also served as the constitution of the Kingdom of God. In it are rules for daily living and rules for dealing with problems arising within the family or community. In it there are rules of how to worship God and how the worship services should be conducted.

God is a God of order; you can see this in his creation. God then instructs his people to make sure they keep these rules in order to set a good example to the nations around them and that all may be well with them.

Deuteronomy 4:6 *"Keep therefore and do them; for this is your wisdom and your understanding in the sight of the nations, which will hear all these statutes, and say, surely this great nation is a wise and understanding people."*

Today the world we live in has gone mad; everyone does what is right in their own eyes. Each man is looking out for himself and selfishness is the order of the day. There are people who are so lonely even though they are among people because society today says you should mind your own business. Everyone is afraid to get involved and many people are distressed and depressed. In the UK, the NHS is spending millions treating people for depression and stress related sicknesses.

The church is therefore supposed to set an example to the world of how the kingdom of God functions; the order, the love and the joy that the people have; the discipline within the family structure and therefore the community and the unity of the people in the bond of love.

God would be their healer, deliverer, and provider and would fight all their battles giving them victory. God would raise up leaders among the people who will rule with wisdom, understanding and righteousness; for when the righteous rule there is peace in the land.

1 Kings 4:29-30, *"And God gave Solomon great wisdom and understanding, and largeness of heart, even as the sand that is on the sea-shore.*

And Solomon's wisdom excelled the wisdom of all the children of the east country, and all the wisdom of Egypt."

When God calls a leader, he also equips them for ruling his inheritance by giving them wisdom. This wisdom is then passed from leader to leader through the generations as long as the leaders were chosen by God and not self appointed or put there by the will of man.

Before Moses died, he had groomed Joshua to take over from him one day, just as Elijah groomed Elisha and Jesus groomed the disciples.

Deuteronomy 34:9, *"And Joshua the son of Nun was full of the spirit of wisdom; for Moses had laid his hands upon him: and the children of Israel hearkened to him, and did as the LORD commanded Moses."*

Wisdom can also be learnt from those whom God has blessed with it as we can see in the story of Job.

Job 33:33, *"Hearken to me: hold thy peace, and I shall teach you wisdom. It is important that when we lack wisdom in dealing with any area of our life we should seek for those whom God has given wisdom or those who have been taught wisdom so we can be counselled."*

Exodus 18:19, *"Hearken now to my voice, I will give you counsel, and God shall be with you"*, for we are told in Pro 15:22 *"Without counsel purposes are disappointed: but in the multitude of counsellors they are established."*

Many people however do not seek counsel when faced with problems and therefore make wrong decisions and their purposes are indeed disappointed. Some people, on the other hand, despise wise counsel to their own destruction.

Proverbs 1:7, *"The fear of the LORD is the beginning of knowledge: but fools despise wisdom and instruction."*

Proverbs 3:13, *"Happy is the man that finds wisdom, and the man that gets understanding."*

To find counselling through God is to accept your place amongst your fellow people, and by offering counselling according to God's guidance, you can share his wisdom and his good example to benefit all of our families and communities.

Have you ever considered creation, how the fish can swim across the open oceans without any guidance yet still reach their destination? What about all the birds that cross countries during different seasons, how do they know which way to fly?

Life is like a maze, and we often need guidance to ensure we reach our destination. God wants to guide man in the same way that he guides the fish in the ocean and the birds in the sky. There are predators along the way, so you need to stay in the group and move along with the protection of others. If you remain behind you may be devoured.

Giving guidance through Godly counselling is the best way to ensure that we all get through this maze together and enjoy the safe and rewarding life that God wants for us all.

Introduction

Isaiah 42:16, *"And I will bring the blind by a way that they knew not; I will lead them in paths that they have not known: I will make darkness light before them, and crooked things straight. These things will I do for them, and not forsake them."*

Isaiah 30:21, *"And your ears shall hear a word behind you, saying, This is the way, walk ye in it, when you turn to the right hand, and when you turn to the left."*

Isaiah 58:11, *"And the LORD will guide you continually, and satisfy your soul in drought, and make fat your bones: and you shall be like a watered garden, and like a spring of water, whose waters fail not."*

We all need peace of mind; this can only come from having a spirit which is free from guilt, anger, bitterness, sorrow and in tune with its maker. When you are at peace, you are indeed like a watered garden, your joy never fails.

Psalm 119:165, *"Great peace have they who love thy law: and nothing shall cause them to stumble."*

I heard a song as I was driving, I don't even know who sang the song but it ministered to my heart. The song says that people need the Lord. At the end of their broken dreams, people need to know somebody cares. This is where a good Christian minister will make a difference to someone's life. People don't need to be lectured or condemned or even reminded of their mistakes, they know it has all gone wrong. What they need is reassurance, acceptance and unconditional love. What they need is someone to make it right again, to clean it all up and give them a second chance and this is what Jesus did.

Jesus cleaned it all up for me and gave me a second chance, and what a difference it has made to my life.

Counselling is an important part of body ministry. Most of us at some point have counselled someone or have been counselled. Maybe you thought you were just giving a word of advice or encouragement. Again every one of us needs guidance at some point in our lives, and the guidance we receive in the form of counselling can make us or break us.

The purpose of Christian counselling is first of all to give spiritual guidance and secondly to produce a Christ like character in individuals, helping them to live a Godly life through making Godly decisions.

The Bible exhorts the ministers of the gospel to use the word of God to:

Encourage

Heb 3:13, *"But exhort one another daily, while it is called To-day; lest any of you be hardened through the deceitfulness of sin."*

We need to challenge one another to do the right things all the time. This is what it means to be my brother's keeper, giving guidance and rebuking in love when it is necessary for the preservation of a soul. You need to be your brother's conscience and the church should be the world's conscience.

Comfort

2 Corithians 1:2-5, *"Grace be to you and peace from God our Father, and from the Lord Jesus Christ.*

Blessed be God, even the Father of our Lord Jesus Christ, the Father of mercies, and the God of all consolation who comforts us in all our tribulations that we may be able to comfort them who are in any trouble by the consolation with which we ourselves are comforted by God.

For as the sufferings of Christ abound in us, so our consolation also abounds by Christ".

Rebuke and Admonish

2 Timothy 4:2, *"Preach the word; be instant in season, out of season; reprove, rebuke, exhort with all long-suffering and doctrine".*

Colossians 3:16, *"Let the word of Christ dwell in you richly in all wisdom; teaching and admonishing one another in psalms, and hymns, and spiritual songs, singing with grace in your hearts to the Lord."*

For the saints to have a Christ-like character they need teaching. Teaching grounds people in the word and helps them to understand Godly principles and a Christian way of life. Christian workers need to be trained for the work of the ministry. Paul said in; 2Ti 3:16-17, *"All scripture is given by inspiration of God, and is profitable for doctrine, for reproof, for correction, for instruction in righteousness".*

That the man of God may be perfect, thoroughly furnished to all good works. Ephesians 4:11-13, *"And he gave some, apostles; and some, prophets; and some, evangelists; and some, pastors and teachers".*

Why did God do this?

For the perfecting of the saints, for the work of the ministry, for the edifying of the body of Christ, until we all come in the unity of the faith, and of the knowledge of the Son of God, to a perfect man, to the measure of the stature of the fullness of Christ.

In the past, a common belief was that a person did not need to be trained as long as they have a calling. Jesus called his disciples, then spent three years of his life training them for the work of the ministry. Training does not necessarily mean one must attend Bible College for three years and get a diploma or certificate, but one can be trained in-house by serving under a trained leader just as Joshua and Elisha did. A person can then receive the necessary impartation and a deeper and more complete understanding of Godly principles. We see this method of training throughout the Bible including the schools of prophets.

Due to the departure from these Godly governing principles, we have seen people destroyed and ship wrecked by well meaning individuals who lacked understanding but were very zealous to offer their advice and teach others. Most of these errors have taken place in the field of counselling, teaching and prophecy, no wonder the Bible warned of using or promoting a novice into the ministry, but the problem is that today anybody can start their own ministry and without accountability to anyone. This is a grievous thing in the sight of God, just as King Saul was told, *"Obedience is better than sacrifice"*, and again God said through the prophet, *"they have run with a message when I have not sent them; if they had waited on me they would have known my ways."* Psalms 25:4, *"Show me thy ways, O LORD; teach me thy paths."*

Counselling is another way of helping people to live disciplined and orderly lives. We are commanded to make disciples of man. God says, "My people perish for lack of knowledge".

Becoming a Christian only gives you power to become Christ-like, you need to then go on to study the word of God in order to follow on, to know him, to know his ways and to gain an understanding of what God requires from his children. Christian life does not exempt you from problems, as some would like to think. On the contrary, when you became born again, only your spirit was born again but your mind and soul still need to be renewed according to the principles of Godly living. You can read my book 'Protecting Your Greatest Asset: Your Mind' for a deeper understanding of how to achieve this.

The book of Romans is full of instructions for all born again believers on how to walk the Christian walk and live the kind of life that is pleasing to God.

The children of this world are much wiser than the children of God because they are instructed on the ways of the world. The kingdom of God has different principles and ways of handling matters than the kingdom of the world. If you can only understand that God is your judge, not the courts of this world, you will then realise why the disciples said to the Jewish elders in Acts 4:19, *"But Peter and John answered and said to them, whether it is right in the sight of God to hearken to you rather than to God, judge ye"*.

It is therefore vital that we have ministers who are qualified to instruct the saints in the ways of God and how to live Godly lives since we have been called to obedience. These principles, however, must first work in your own life before you can teach them to others, Like a driving instructor, you must be qualified to drive the car and have many years of experience before you can teach others, otherwise they will learn your mistakes and the result will be disastrous. Learning to drive gives you a set of skills, but then you need a different set of skills to pass your expertise on to others. Not only do you have to learn how to drive, you also have to learn how to teach.

In the book of Leviticus, God gave instructions to Israel about the Priesthood. There were certain things which disqualified individuals from ministering before God, even though they had that right by birth.

Leviticus 21:18-23, *"For whatever man he may be that hath a blemish, he shall not approach: a blind man, or a lame, or he that hath a flat nose, or any thing superfluous. Or a man that is broken-footed, or broken-handed, or crooked-backed, or a dwarf, or that hath a blemish in his eye, or be scurvy, or scabbed, or hath his peculiar members broken: No man of the seed of Aaron the priest, that hath a blemish, shall come nigh to offer the offerings of the LORD made by fire; he hath a blemish, he shall not come nigh to offer the bread of his God. He shall eat the bread of his God, both of the most holy, and of the holy. Only he shall not go in to the Vail, nor come nigh to the altar, because he hath a blemish; that he may not profane my sanctuaries: for I the LORD do sanctify them."*

You may be a Christian but if you have a blemish you may open your own church or presume to be a minister of the Gospel, and man may accept you but God will not. These blemishes were natural for Israel but for today's believers these are spiritual blemishes.

The blemishes described in Leviticus may not seem relevant today, yet we can equate them to qualities or spiritual blemishes which would disqualify someone from ministering before God and offering Godly counselling.

Blindness: Lacking understanding of spiritual truths, having no revelation, this is the result of not being born again.

Lameness: Having problems with your spiritual walk, always stumbling and falling over issues, always picking up offences.

A Flat Nose: Lack of discernment, lack of sensitivity to the presence of God.

Superflousness: To have an extra body part such as finger or toe. A person who is not properly planted or committed to a local church. Lack of submission, drawing attention to oneself. Also means someone without the word of truth.

A broken foot: An unfaithful person, not trust worthy, Proverbs 25:19, *"Confidence in an unfaithful man in time of trouble is like a broken tooth, and a foot out of joint."*

A Broken Hand: Lacking a servant's heart and having no liberty in giving or being a blessing to others.

Crooked Back: Being spineless, lacking a backbone, constantly having a 'poor me' mentality. Failure to look up or stand up and be counted.

A Dwarf: One who stopped growing spiritually, never reached their potential. Lack of maturity. Narrow minded and small hearted.

Blemish in the eye: Failing to keep unity, failing to submit or keep rank. Unsteady or double minded.

Scurvy: To have the itch, under pressure to do something, can't wait got to do it now. God's emphasis is on BEING not DOING.

Broken stones: Inability to produce, inability to perform or follow through or to fulfil.

Scabbiness: Always picking up other people's offences.

(Taken From the School Of Ministry Training Series "A", by Gordon William Schuetz. p13-14)

Satellite Navigation as a Picture of Spiritual Guidance

One evening, my husband and I were travelling to another city to attend a wedding. Since we didn't know the route, we borrowed a friend's satellite navigation system, or SatNav. It was difficult sometimes to know where to turn, even with the SatNav's instructions. When faced with a roundabout, the SatNav would say, "in 200 meters bear left and immediately take the third exit".

Firstly how do you measure 200 meters? Secondly we discovered that the SatNav did not consider some of the exits but only the major ones. The fact that we were not familiar with this SatNav made things worse.

We took many wrong turns and the SatNav would say, "please turn around at the next junction" and it would redirect us again. At one point we travelled a very long distance and the SatNav was very quiet, so I thought the battery had gone flat or we had lost the signal. Then suddenly it would say, "at the next round about take the second exit". This was fine until we found ourselves in the middle of nowhere, in the dark and with no street lights. We began to panic, wondering, "what if we are lost?", "what if the battery runs out?", and, "what if we lose the signal?" We had no idea where we were and had taken so many turns we could never find our way forward or backward. We had completely come to depend on the SatNav.

Have you ever been in this situation, spiritually or emotionally, where there was no way backward nor forward, trapped in your circumstances? It's a very frightening place to find yourself.

Eventually we came back onto a main road, and after a short distance we could see the venue that we were going to.

This experience got me thinking about the Holy Spirit and how he guides us everyday through this life. How gently, unchanging, uncompromising he is, the same today yesterday and forever. There are however times when we are not sure he knows what he is doing, times when we question the wisdom of leading us a certain way. There are times when we choose not to follow his guidance to our own destruction but when we do, he picks us up and tells us the next step forward. When we go the wrong way, he urges us to turn around in repentance to start again where we left the way. Like the SatNav, he does not condemn, judge or ridicule, he treats you as if the mistake never happened. He never offers his opinion, simply giving you guidance. If you choose not to follow, he can't do anything as it's your choice. After going around in circles, when you decide to listen he just picks up from there and redirects you back to the route that will take you in the right direction. His patience is infinite.

Recently we travelled to another city we have never visited before to attend a women's retreat. Again the venue was in a rural area.

This trip was worse than the first one, we went round in circles for a whole hour because we would not trust the SatNav, it told us to turn into a road which we thought was wrong because it had a name which we did not associate with the direction we were heading.

After a whole hour of driving round and ending up in the same place, after all the calls made for advice and direction had failed, we finally decided to follow the SatNav and amazingly this was, after all, the right route.

Immediately we got onto the right road and the SatNav said "carry on until further directions", meaning that we would travel a long distance on the same route without having to worry about turning off. You would think that we had learnt our lesson, yet when we came to another rural area and the SatNav told us to turn left, we decided to turn around as we couldn't see a turning. The SatNav immediately told us to make a 'U turn' which we eventually did and continued forward in the darkness only to find there was a small narrow road which took us to our destination.

I began to meditate on these experiences and relate them to how the Holy Spirit like a SatNav, patiently tries to guide us on our journey of life. But due to lack of trust which comes from our ignorance of his abilities we choose to go our own way. Often, if we cannot immediately see the wisdom of his guidance, it is too easy to ignore it.

There are times when we are confused by the many voices of other people that we get even more confused and more lost. We get confused more by the people who we assume have the answer or know what they are doing, yet sadly we sometimes realise too late that they are as lost as we are. Every time we were on the right route and there was a long stretch, the SatNav was quiet. There are times when God seems to be very quiet, so you pray and ask for directions and he seems to say nothing. It is during such times that you need to remain stable, doing what you are doing without making any changes.

The trouble is that most of us are like Abram and Sarai; they made their move when they thought God was taking to long.

The Bible says: Isaiah 40:31 *"But they that wait upon the LORD shall renew their strength; they shall mount up with wings as eagles; they shall run, and not be weary; they shall walk, and not faint"*.

It is important to understand your SatNav if it will be useful to you. The SatNav can only be as good as the information you feed into it, but it is fit for purpose. If you abide in Christ and his word abides in you, then you will get to know and understand him, and this will cause you to trust him. If you trust him then you will be able to follow where he leads even if sometimes it doesn't immediately seem right in your own mind or those of your friends.

Daniel 11:32b *"But the people that know their God shall be strong, and do exploits"*.

What is Counselling?

Counselling is encouraging believers to look at their problems through God's word and to seek solutions which glorify God and bring peace and harmony in their relationship to God first and to others. Christian counselling must be based on biblical principles.

Counselling happens when a counsellor offers and agrees to give their time and attention to listen to another person's problems and then facilitates by giving the individual an opportunity to explore, discover and clarify issues with the view of coming up with Godly outcomes.

A counsellor therefore needs to be able to listen, observe and respond well.

Effective counselling must have the following attributes:

Wisdom

A counsellor must have understanding; the ability to see the individual's world through that individual's eyes and then help them to turn around and see the same world through the word of God.

Respect

A counsellor must have an attitude of respecting others and recognising their right to privacy, confidentiality and indeed freedom of choice. God never forces anyone to believe his word or to do what he says.

Being specific

A counsellor must take care not to give a double message and confuse the person. A counsellor must be clear and direct, and the trap here is the fear of hurting someone's feelings, thereby failing to be truthful and honest. A good counsellor is specific, honest and tactful.

Genuineness

A counsellor must be real; people need to know they can trust you and value your advice. Be honest and don't pretend to have all the answers. Speak the truth at all times, yet remember however that truth spoken without love does more harm than good. Counselling is not an opportunity for you to share your problems too, it is an opportunity for you to listen with an open mind and guide only according to the wisdom of God.

Congruence

A counsellor's words must match their lifestyle, not a case of 'do what I say, not what I do'. Never manipulate the word of God in order to achieve an outcome.

Equally, a counsellor must not be 'perfect' either. You are not a role model for how to live your life; you are a role model for how to work every day towards being a better person in the Kingdom of God.

Insight

There are two types of problems which you will meet as a counsellor; problems of misunderstandings and those of emotional or mental issues.

In order to understand the nature of the problem you need to ask the right questions. People normally do not tell you the real issue either because they genuinely do not know or they are in denial or embarrassed. Sometimes, the mind blocks certain painful events as a coping mechanism although this will not deal with the root cause. Each person develops a coping mechanism, some wear masks to cover their true feelings while others turn to alcohol or drugs. For example, someone may seem very talkative because they fear silence, someone else may work constantly and be seen as very hard working because they don't want to stop and think. People often find ways to cope with their problems that appear normal, so a good counsellor will see past these coping mechanisms and understand the person's true feelings and fears.

Case Study

I counselled a couple once who had previously received unwise counselling. The wife was very unwell and I suspected that this was to do with HIV/AIDS. I arranged a meeting with both husband and wife; they did not talk about this subject but rather explained that she was unwell. This lady had been diagnosed as having Tuberculosis, she was then counselled to believe in God for her healing and not take any medication. She had actually refused treatment at the hospital with the support of her counsellor.

First of all I asked her if she had been to see her doctor, and this is when the full story came out. I asked her if she felt that accepting treatment was a sin, and she revealed that she had been encouraged to stand on faith and not give in, so this was what she was doing. I sensed in my spirit that she did not have faith but was actually driven by fear of what would happen if she wavered. I asked her what she thought was wrong with her and she wavered in her reply. I asked if they had considered having an HIV test done and they both said, "no". I asked, "why not?" since her symptoms were pointing that way.

The couple said they were afraid to be tested for HIV. I explained that it would be better to rule this out and also to visit a doctor and allow them to investigate the cause of the illness, since it was not getting any better. I also explained that God was not against doctors or medical treatment, and that receiving treatment did not indicate a lack of faith or weakness. This couple was obviously afraid of facing the prospect of HIV but I had a strong feeling that they knew what was wrong all along. I explained that HIV can be successfully controlled and that one can go on to live a very long life under medication, therefore they need not die like fools. I am a great believer in healing and I have actually prayed for people with cancer and they were healed and certified by doctors. I have prayed for barren women and they conceived and I have seen people delivered from demonic oppression, so I know that God heals. I have also prayed for some people and they were not healed, but don't ask me why some are healed and some are not because only God knows the answer to this question. When healing is God's will, I can show the way and give that person the right guidance and direction, but if it is not God's will then no-one can know the reason for that. It is not because the person has sinned, because God can forgive, so there is no need for anyone to fear if prayer does not work.

Unfortunately for this couple, by this time the wife was very poorly and had to be taken to hospital by ambulance. The doctors asked if they would like an HIV test to be done and they agreed. The test came back positive. The hospital battled to save the wife but lost the battle. While this couple was supposed to believe God for their healing, there were many other issues between them that needed dealing with. The husband went on to get treatment and survived.

It is helpful to know what kind of questions to use in order for someone to open up about their fears so that you can then advise, encourage and support them to take the right steps.

This terrible mistake happened due to lack of understanding biblical principles. Zeal without knowledge can be very dangerous, and good intentions are not always enough when there is a risk of placing someone's life at risk. It is also necessary to understand that people have different levels of faith and you can not force faith on anyone. Faith has to grow through exercise and experience.

As a counsellor you will also need to have a good understanding of Scriptures, using the Word in counselling, dealing with grief and dealing with guilt.

A misunderstanding of the word leads to misguided counselling which can destroy lives as in the case above. Remember that as a counsellor, you are not the expert in the person's life, and you are not the holder of all the right answers. You are a guide, and you must counsel with an open mind in order to guide the person to God's will. You can not tell the person what they should do, you can only ever give them the space, permission and support to explore every possibility for themselves.

Psalm 119:165, *"Great peace have they who love thy law: and nothing shall cause them to stumble."*

Psalm 37:23, *"The steps of a good man are ordered by the LORD: and he takes delight in his way."*

As a counsellor, you need to know issues of salvation, repentance, confession and forgiveness as well as understanding biblical principles. You need to find your solutions from the word of God not the wisdom of man.

A counsellor should have a prayer life and a relationship with the spirit. The Holy Spirit will give you Godly wisdom and can even help you to discern the hidden things of the heart. Remember, scripture says, "The heart is evil above all things who can know it".

When counselling anyone, the first point of call should be the issue of salvation and establishing the authority of God's word in the individual's life. If someone is not saved, they will not understand or be governed by the word of God so you might have to use Godly wisdom in advising and guiding them.

One thing you will soon learn is that people don't always tell the truth. When dealing with more than one person it is not wise to listen to only one side of the story as you might find out later that you did not get an accurate picture of things. Each person is right in their own eyes and will present what is truth to them. This is why Godly wisdom and understanding is a must if you wish to become a good counsellor.

Sometimes people lie or bend the truth to protect their own interests, and sometimes they lie out of love for someone else. Hiding the truth will make counselling impossible, because it is like trying to lead the person out of a maze when you yourself can't see where all the walls are.

1 Corinthians 1:18, *"For the preaching of the cross is to them that perish, foolishness; but to us who are saved, it is the power of God."*

Romans 8:7, *"Because the carnal mind is enmity against God: for it is not subject to the law of God, neither indeed can be."*

The first goal of Christian counselling is to check the spiritual condition of the individual. You need to know whether Christ is Lord in the person's life because if he is not, your Godly counsel will be wasted. If the ruler-ship of Christ has not been established in the person's life, this will be, like Jesus said, throwing your pearls to swine. If their heart is closed, the word of God will do nothing for them.

You also need to be sensitive towards people harbouring bitterness or unforgiveness. If not dealt with, it will block any progress. Unforgiveness can be the underlying factor to many bodily torments, health problems and mental anguish. Doctors have long known the serious health effects of stress, and unforgiveness places a great deal of stress on a person.

Whatever the person knows in their mind will always be affected by the pain they feel in their heart.

We are advised by the writer of Hebrews 12:14, *"Follow peace with all men, and holiness, without which no man shall see the Lord."*

We also need to take heed of John's warning, 1 John 3:15, *"Whoever hates his brother, is a murderer: and ye know that no murderer hath eternal life abiding in him."*

Counselling is a wonderful gift which will help people find their way back onto the path of God, and as a Godly counsellor, you will know the important role that you have played in the lives of the people you counsel.

USING THE WORD IN COUNSELLING

Proper understanding of the word of God will help you as a counsellor. Paul urged Timothy to study the word in order to show himself approved, rightly dividing the word of truth.

2 Timothy 2:15, *"Study to show thyself approved to God, a workman that needs not to be ashamed, rightly dividing the word of truth."*

In the case study of the couple suffering from HIV, the previous counsellor let the couple down, because if the counselling had been wise, the wife would not have died. Don't ever assume that everyone is at the same level, spiritually. Faith is like a muscle, it needs to be exercised slowly before one can attempt to believe in God for big things.

Sometimes you will come across someone who is angry with God. They may be asking, "Why is God doing this to me?" or "Why does God allow suffering in the world?"

It is not wise for one to attempt to explain why an individual is suffering unless it is obvious that their suffering is due to a sinful lifestyle. Remember Job's comforters; we know that the cause of suffering is not always due to sin.

Once, the disciples asked Jesus about a disabled man. They wanted to know who had sinned for this man to be this way; was it his parents or the man himself? Jesus answered them by saying that neither this man nor his parents had sinned.

Job 1:8, *"And the LORD said to Satan, Hast thou considered my servant Job, that there is none like him on the earth, a perfect and an upright man, one that fears God, and shuns evil?"*

And yet Job suffered so much that his friends were sure that God was punishing him for some evil he had done.

People have a misconception that true Christians should not suffer, giving the impression that those who suffer are not genuine Christians or that there is something wrong with what they are doing. This kind of thinking only makes the suffering person more angry and confused. Remember, God is love and he does not take pleasure in the suffering of man or in the death of a sinner.

2 Timothy 2:12, *"If we suffer, we shall also reign with him: if we deny him, he also will deny us."*

1 Peter 2:19, *"For this is thank-worthy, if a man for conscience towards God endures grief, suffering wrongfully."*

1 Peter 2:20, *"For what glory is it, if, when you are buffeted for your faults, you bear it patiently? but if, when you do well, and suffer for it, you bear it patiently, this is acceptable with God."*

1 Peter 2:21, *"For even to this were you called: because Christ also suffered for us, leaving us an example, that we should follow his steps."*

Dealing with grief

Particular attention is needed towards those who are grieving, whether it's the loss of a loved one, job or anything that is important to them. Remember that it's their loss, not yours, even though it may seem trivial to you. Be very careful as trivialising someone's pain might result in hurting them further, the Bible says an offended brother is harder to win back. If you accidentally do this, you can easily lose the trust that this person has placed in you and you can lose your opportunity to counsel them.

With grief or negative news might come shock and denial. Be careful of those who may not show any emotion as some people internalise their feelings and you will see their pain and stress showing in other ways.

When I was growing up as a Christian, we were told that we should not grieve when we lose our loved ones because the Bible says that we should not grieve as the world grieves. This left people to bottle up their grief which ate away at them like a cancer.

The Bible did not say that we should not grieve, grieving is a natural process which when handled well, aids the healing process. What that scripture means is that although we mourn, we are comforted by the fact that we know that our loved one is in Christ and we shall meet again. When we grieve for someone, we know that they are now at peace and are no longer tormented, whereas the world believes that death is an end and the world therefore grieves with no comforter.

We grieve for what the person has left behind in the world, we grieve for our own loss, but we need not grieve for our loved one's soul.

We know that when you die without salvation you go to a place of torment. There is no peace and your fate is worse than anything you can imagine here on Earth and this is for eternity.

Paul said that for me to live is Christ and to die is a gain because I will then be present with my Lord, this is where our comfort lies.

Asking the right questions and showing empathy may draw the person into discussing their deepest hurts, so also bear in mind that some physical and behavioural problems can have emotional roots.

Grieving can sometimes link with loneliness and can therefore present as depression where the person might be saying to you, "I feel like God has abandoned me". Grieving can also be accompanied by guilt which in most cases the person fails to shake off. The person might be saying to you, "I don't know why I am depressed but I can't seem to shake it off" because their guilt over something that they did or did not do can never go away, because now their loved one is gone and they have no second chance. Therefore, you must deal with the person's feelings of loss, not with what it is that they should or should not have done or said.

In counselling there is no one size that fits all. People who fail to deal with grief in the right way open themselves to demonic invasion; this is where ancestral worship, spiritualism and other similar practices originate from. When someone dies and the living relative has some guilt due to unresolved issues or a simple failure to let go, the person's spirit becomes an easy target for demonic operation as they begin to seek the dead in their dreams or visit spiritualists and fortune tellers in order to connect with the dead person, and the Devil will certainly accommodate them.

Ecclesiastes 9:5-6, *"For the living know that they shall die: but the dead know not any thing, neither have they any more a reward; for the memory of them is forgotten. Also their love, and their hatred, and their envy, has now perished; neither have they any more a portion for ever in any thing that is done under the sun."*

The Bible says that the dead have nothing to do with the living any more.

Isaiah 8:1, *"And when they shall say to you, Seek to them that have familiar spirits, and to wizards that peep, and that mutter: should not a people seek to their God? for the living to the dead?"*

Leviticus 19:31, *"Regard not them that have familiar spirits, neither seek after wizards, to be defiled by them: I am the LORD your God."*

1 Chronicles 10:13, *"So Saul died from his transgression which he committed against the Lord, even against the word of the Lord, which*

he kept not, and also for asking counsel of one that had a familiar spirit, to enquire of it."

God hates these things and we are warned not to partake in these sinful behaviours of worshipping or communicating with the dead. Your knowledge and correct use of the word of God can save a soul from perishing due to ignorance.

Twenty years ago when my father died, I was a young but very prayerful Christian. I was involved in the ministry of deliverance within the church. I began to have dreams about my father which were very real. At first I entertained these dreams because I was very close to my father. But then I began to question these dreams as I thought about the scriptures quoted above. I took this confusion to God in prayer and felt in my spirit the Lord was saying that when I have the next encounter with my father, I should rebuke that spirit in the name of Jesus. I did exactly that and the image of my father disappeared in a puff of smoke.

The Lord then explained to me that this was how the Devil deceives people into believing his demons were their dead relatives. This is the root of all spiritualism, ancestral worship and paganism. My father owned businesses, and my sister still worked in one of them.

At the back of the shop, there was a water leak somewhere which the water meter was showing but because the whole yard was covered with concrete, the City Council workers had to dig up the yard in order to find the leaking pipe.

My sister had a visitation from my "father" who told her exactly where the leaking pipe was. In the morning she told the workers where to dig and, sure enough, she was right. Those men wanted to know how she was able to pin point the exact spot but she told them she had just sensed it. My sister was a church goer but was not really keen on the things of God so she was very excited about this. When she told me, I told her what to do and she had the same experience as I did. Until you are convinced about the word of God you will never be able to convince others. Most of what the world calls the sixth sense is actually a manifestation of demonic influence.

The Lord allowed me to have these experiences because of the deliverance ministry which he has given to me. He wanted me to understand where all these misunderstandings come from. People worship the dead because they have had "genuine" experience talking with the dead, unfortunately what they do not know is that they have been deceived and are entertaining evil spirits.

The Bible speaks of familiar spirits; these spirits are familiar with your surroundings and everything pertaining to you. When you die, they wear a mask that looks like you and they put on your voice and speak like you. They are very good imitators. If you do not believe me, watch the movie industry very closely and you will see what I mean.

Some years ago I met a lady who had an encounter with a spiritualist which put fear into her life but at the same time opened her understanding of the demonic world. She was invited by a friend to attend a spiritualist meeting. Some people asked to speak to their dead relatives and they would speak to them, so she asked to speak to Jesus. A figure appeared dressed in the way in which Jesus is always portrayed by the church. She got so excited that she asked him, "Lord show me the nail scars on your hands", and to everyone's surprise this spirit became angry and disappeared. This lady was so shaken at first but later realised that this was not Jesus which is why he could not show the scars on his hands.

If someone comes for counselling and tells you that their dead relative is coming to them in dreams and telling them things that are real and you say to them that this is only their imagination, it is not real, you will not be able to help the person because they know what they have experienced, and it seems so real to them. The Bible warns us not to believe every spirit but to test the spirits. Sometimes people might be having demonic visitations and they think it is God. It can be very difficult to convince someone that the spirit which is showing them these things is actually an evil spirit, as the Bible warns us that Satan sometimes pretends to be the angel of light; which is why we are encouraged to test the spirits and not just believe every manifestation.

In the church, I have so often seen situations where a familiar spirit pretends to be a prophet of God and many lives are wrecked and destroyed as they believe the lie. A few years ago I was asking my Lord in prayer saying, "Lord, you said this and this will happen, now I have been waiting for years faithfully, when is this prophecy going to be fulfilled?" I was concerned because I was growing older and still nothing. The answer was that God will bring his Word to pass for he is not a man that he should lie but if he did not promise it, it will never come to pass for you have believed a lie, you have been deceived and turned away from the path which God had prepared for you.

Many, like me, have believed a lie from the pits of hell and were diverted from the path they should have followed or wasted time waiting for something which will never happen. Many even married wrong partners because somebody prophesied that this is what the Lord is saying. There is so much witchcraft in the field of prophecy due to familiar spirits which is the spirit behind false prophets. It's a controlling spirit which can also have influence in counselling.

I am reminded of a young evangelist who was so zealous for God and was operating in gifts. One day a lady in their church gave him "a word from the Lord", he was told that God wanted him to take over the pastorship from the existing pastor because that pastor had failed God. This young man was obviously spiritually immature and believed that this was of God. Perhaps that's what his heart had desired, after all the Bible says every man is tempted after their own lust. I explained to this young man that the word was definitely not from God as God does not operate in that fashion. God is not the author of confusion. If this pastor was failing, the prophecy would have been directed to the pastor himself and God would have spoken to the young man to prepare him for what was to come. This is how God operated when dethroning Saul and anointing David. This prophecy destroyed the church and the young evangelist's ministry ended there as well.

As a counsellor, you must often balance worldly knowledge with the wisdom of God. You must choose between what often seem to be hard facts and real evidence, and what you know in your heart to be the true Will of God.

God's will always prevails, and the only question is how difficult we will make the journey for ourselves.

As a Godly counsellor, you can show how to make the journey more straightforward, yet it is still up to the person to choose to follow that path.

Dealing with guilt

Guilt can cause problems if not recognised and dealt with effectively. Remember, people will often present you with the fruit of their problem and it is your duty as a counsellor to help them identify the root. Dealing with the symptoms will only delay the inevitable and will not solve the problem. As a counsellor, you will need to know how to present the truth without condemning or laying blame.

Usually, when someone refuses to accept the wrong they have done, they will blame everyone else for what has gone wrong in their lives. You will see their own guilt revealed in their anger and frustration, because by misdirecting their own guilt onto other people, they can never address the cause of it, and they become more and more frustrated. You need to be able to help the person to come to terms with the truth and own up to their own guilt so that they can take responsibility for the mistakes they have made. When you talk to drug addicts or alcoholics, they will often blame someone or something for how they turned out; usually their upbringing, their parents, wives, husbands, loss of employment, anything but facing up to the fact that they made a mistake somewhere along the way.

When people lie to themselves so many times for such a long time they end up believing their own lies and things just get worse. Finding the root of the problem is not easy but can be done prayerfully, and the Holy Spirit can give guidance when we ask for it.

The book of Proverbs is full of wisdom.

Proverbs 15:2, *"The tongue of the wise use knowledge rightly: but the mouth of fools pours out foolishness."*

Proverbs 19:20, *"Hear counsel, and receive instruction, that you may be wise in your latter end."*

Life is about decision making, therefore decisions have to be reached. In making decisions, consideration must be given to the effect of those decisions on the wider family. Motives must be examined, such as "Why take this step?", "Is this honouring God and his word?", "Has consideration been made of others likely to be affected by this decision", and, "Have all other options been considered?"

Often, the person will be afraid to explore every possibility because there are some courses of action that they rule out at the beginning of the process. For example, if someone is experiencing problems in a relationship, they might refuse to explore the possibility of ending the relationship through fear of loss and the unknown. However, they must explore every option in order to reach the right decision. If it is not the right choice then at least they have explored it sensibly and honestly and not been closed minded.

Often, a situation is made into a problem by a feeling of being trapped, so by exploring every option, even the unthinkable ones, the person is no longer trapped by what they can or cannot do, they are now taking responsibility for making a free choice. Choosing to stay in a situation and put it right is better than having to put it right because you cannot leave.

Every decision made must reflect Christian values and principles as well as the rights and needs of others. This also applies to Christian discipline within the church.

1 Timothy 5:8, *"But if any provides not for his own, and especially for those of his own house, he has denied the faith, and is worse than an infidel."*

People can be very selfish and self centred. Consider people who commit suicide and ask, what is the driving force? Mostly they want to hurt those who have hurt them or make them feel guilty for the way they treated them. Depression feeds on self pity, and people with self pity focus on themselves and what they want and can't have. They focus on the wrongs that have been done to them and their own emotional pain, not seeing the pain they may have caused others.

Deal with all forms of selfishness and self centredness as these are the fruits of the flesh and displease God. Decisions must never be arrived at without deliberation as the impact of our choices will affect our relationship with God and with others and will open the door to guilt. "If your conscience condemns you not then you have peace with God".

Always be aware of half truths and self deception and be willing to challenge this in an appropriate manner. There is a great need for honesty in exposing sin and calling it by its name and we are instructed by the word of God on how to change our circumstances. The Holy Spirit gives us the ability or power to make the right choices if we are in submission to Him. Suicide is not the answer, for the Bible says cursed is he who hangs on a tree. If you take your own life you will end up in hell. Life is precious; it was not your decision to be born therefore you don't choose when to depart either. Hell is very real and it is no alternative to dealing openly and honestly with guilt.

DEALING WITH NEGATIVITY

A negative mindset can be very difficult to deal with, and a person who has allowed themselves to dwell in this mindset for too long will find it hard to let go of it. Many people who are very negative have low self esteem or a poor self image. They believe the worst about themselves and therefore others. They are often paranoid, thinking that people speak negatively about them. Due to this mindset, they are unable to make or keep friends, they wear out anyone who tries to befriend them and they can end up as loners. The real danger with this is that they can end up in depression or very angry with society and become self destructive or will turn and destroy others.

These people occasionally meet people of like mind who will encourage each other to do bad things as they feel the world owes them and therefore they want to punish those who seem to be happier than they are. It is important as a counsellor to be able to identify this and deal with it effectively. This mindset may be due to someone whose confidence has been knocked down by constant criticism or failure to achieve something that's important to the person. Hope deferred also makes someone begin to doubt their capabilities or they begin to think something is wrong with them. This, if unchecked, can develop into paranoia.

I know of a young man who was very handsome, very gifted and could have achieved anything he set his mind to achieve. This young man simply allowed childhood foolish anger to get out of hand. He made friends with a group of boys and they started a project together. The project was going well but he began to feel that the others were doing better than him. Instead of appreciating their differences and the contribution they all brought together, complementing one another, he began to feel insecure. When the project was completed it did not go as well as was anticipated and this only made things worse. This young person lost all confidence in his abilities and his self doubt began to grow.

He now lost confidence in himself and began to feel very negative about himself. He could not make any new friends and wallowed in his self pity. This is a sad place to be in and people in this situation don't see a way out of it and can lose hope of changing their circumstances. A defeated spirit comes upon them and they go into depression and don't want to get out of bed, work or do anything. They literally have no direction or desire to do anything, saying, "What's the point? I am only going to mess up again". The sad thing is that some of these people will turn to drugs and alcohol for comfort.

Why do people come to this point? A competitive spirit is one reason. When you fail to achieve your goals you can come to despise those who do achieve theirs, yet deep inside you despise yourself for being a failure. This is why it is important for a person to understand who they are and what they want to do with their lives and not compare themselves to other people. When you are secure in your own self you will not feel threatened by other peoples' successes. Sometimes. even the most secure people will go through these emotions, so it is important to face these emotions and deal with them correctly.

As a counsellor, you will need to understand what is going on in the person's mind and encourage them to see it too. If they can admit to having these emotions and be willing to deal with them they will be well on the road to recovery.

Counselling Techniques

Counselling is a very important part of ministering and should be planned for. It should take place in a secure environment which also provides dignity, privacy and confidentiality.

There are times when counselling will be informal, involving easy problems needing a straightforward decision based on Godly wisdom. For an arranged counselling session, you need to prepare yourself spiritually by praying before hand.

Put aside at least one hour with no disturbance so that you can give all of your attention to the individual. This also shows that you are serious about their problem and that they have your complete attention. Make sure that there will be no interruptions. Get someone else to answer the phone or the door.

As a counsellor, you need to have listening skills, as in Proverbs 18:13, *"He that answers a matter before he hear it, it is foolishness and shame to him."*

James 1:19, *"Therefore, my beloved brethren, let every man be swift to hear, slow to speak, slow to anger."*

A counsellor must show interest in what is being said and offer empathy and understanding, as told in Romans 12:15, *"Rejoice with them that rejoice, and weep with them that weep."*

A counsellor must have good probing skills, be able to use questions well and know when to interrupt the conversation, as in:

Proverbs 20:5, *"Counsel in the heart of man is like deep water; but a man of understanding will draw it out."*

Only interrupt when appropriate, paraphrase what has been said to press home the point. Summarise what has been said to clarify and then move forward.

Use prompts to encourage continuity and try to draw out their feelings, and be very observant of their body language. Show understanding by nodding where appropriate and don't let silence unsettle you. Use the space to reflect and observe body language and listen to the Holy Spirit. Remember, he is the counsellor, let him counsel through you and again he is the comforter so let him comfort through you. Help to keep the focus on both present and past as they might be links, and watch out for inconsistencies and gently point them out.

Make sure that there are clear goals and actions before ending the session.

You need to keep a record of your session, what was said, what was agreed and what will be discussed at the next meeting and give support were necessary to accomplish the goals. Pray to close the session and remember to give relevant scripture to take home. When goals have been achieved, your notes must be securely destroyed. Unlike professional psychological counselling or psychotherapy, Christian counselling is not a business but a ministry which is given as part of pastoral care, therefore there is no need to keep any counselling records as we are not dealing with clients but brethren. Always remember that confidentiality is vital, otherwise people will not trust you in the future.

What type of questions to ask

Sometimes you may not quite see what the problem is, or the problem may be so complex that it is hard to know which area to start with. You need to look at all aspects of life such as family background, relationships, employment, finances, spiritual life, sexual life, marital life, health, recreation and sense of responsibility. Life is like a wheel with all the areas of life interconnected. When one area is out of tune, the whole wheel is pushed out of balance.

Remember, this is not a church sermon and you are not there to preach but to counsel, so avoid preaching to the individual. Give biblical facts and let the individual apply them to their situation. In the past, some counsellors literally told the person what they should do or say. This is treating an individual like a baby who can not reason, and this is where power and control became a problem as leaders made people so dependent on them for everything that in the end they owned and controlled the person. God never called upon us to control peoples' lives but rather to equip people and help them to grow and mature with the ability and wisdom to make the right decisions based on scriptural principles. You are there to help them find guidance, not to tell them what to do.

Often, it is most useful to remember that the person is not asking for help because they don't know what to do, therefore you don't have to tell them what to do. They are often asking for help because they already know what they have to do, but they are struggling with the consequences of that decision. They are struggling with their conscience or guilt, their self doubt or fear. Nothing that you can tell them to do will resolve that, only the guidance that you can find in the Bible will help them to make sense of their choices.

Make sure the individual understands that, while you are counselling them, they should not be receiving counsel elsewhere as this will bring confusion. It is good that they seek advice to help with their decisions, but they must invest in one counselling relationship as much as you will invest in them.

Above all, you must not tolerate a person who goes from one counsellor to the next, hoping to get the answers that they want to hear. If they don't agree, they blame the counsellor and move on to the next. Often, they just want someone to listen to them, and it is as if they are addicted to counselling. This is the true nature of their problem, not whatever they present to you. Always begin a counselling relationship by asking the person if they have sought counselling in the past.

You need to help the individual to set up short and long term goals and recommend relevant scripture to meditate on at home. If you are not the pastor of this individual, you need to first find out if they have been counselled by their pastor to ensure that you will not be contradicting the council given by the pastor who has spiritual oversight over their life. If they have and there are discrepancies, you could, with their permission, check the facts. Sometimes, people would try to deceive you into supporting them with whatever they intend to do so they have someone to blame when it all goes wrong. Some people seek comfort in their problems through attention, and they will draw many people into their self pity, changing their story slightly each time to get the most attention. Don't be part of the confusion but be part of the solution.

Remember these four areas when counselling:

1. What is the person saying is the problem? If dealing with more than one person, what is the other person saying is the problem?

2. Has the person been counselled before? If so, by whom and what advice were they given?

3. What are they expecting from this counselling, or what are they hoping to achieve through your counselling which they did not achieve before?

4. Did they find the session useful, and do they want another session?

As a counsellor, you are not there to tell them what to do but to guide a process of self reflection so they can see what the real problem is and discover their own solution.

Remember, unless a person can see the root of the problem for themselves they will not be able to resolve it. If they are in denial, you will have to work harder at making them see the problem so that they can decide what they wish to do with it.

People need to own the solution so that they can mature and then move forward but if you tell them what to do they will never think for themselves and the lesson will never be learned. You will compound their tendency to blame others for their situation.

Fear and anger

When counselling, you need to be aware of fear and anger. These emotions are usually the root causes of many other presenting problems which affect relationships as well as mental and physical health.

Fear is the root of phobias while anger is the root of anti-social behaviour. Fear also causes anxiety and worry. The Bible says of anger, in Ecclesiastes 7:9, *"Anger rests in the bosom of fools"*.

Matthew challenged the believers by taking this a step further;

Mat 5:22-24, *"But I say to you, That whoever is angry with his brother without a cause, shall be in danger of the judgement: and whoever shall say to his brother, Raca, shall be in danger of the council: but whoever shall say, Thou fool, shall be in danger of hell-fire. Therefore when you bring your gift to the altar, and there remember that your brother has something against you, Leave there your gift before the altar, and go your way; first be reconciled to your brother, and then come and offer your gift."*

Remember that internalised anger can give birth to bitterness, resentment, unforgiveness, depression, suicidal feelings and guilt. People can be angry against God or others, even if their anger is misplaced. Mostly, people feel they have a right to be angry and often, their anger is really at themselves. When a person is angry, they are often blaming someone else, yet it is they who must often seek forgiveness first before they can let go of their anger.

You can tell from a conversation when someone is angry with someone else by observing their body language when they talk about that person. It is so vital for a counsellor to have observational skills as well as discernment. Remember, it is not wrong to be angry. The Bible actually says that it is acceptable to be angry but don't let the sun go down while you are still angry, meaning that if you do not deal with your anger quickly, it will grow and grow to a point where you can no longer control it.

What the Bible says about fear

Job 3:25-26, *"For the thing which I greatly feared has come upon me, and that which I dreaded has come to me. I was not in safety, neither had I rest, neither was I quiet; yet trouble came."*

Psalms 56:3-4, *"In the time when I am afraid, I will trust in thee."*

In God I will praise his word, in God I have put my trust; I will not fear what flesh can do to me. Remember, the Bible says that the fear of man is a snare.

When counselling someone who has fear, you need to understand that their fear is very real to them. Help them to identify the root cause and then deal with it. I once met someone who would not allow themselves to love anyone. They became very abusive of others, using people and discarding them when they were finished with them.

The root of this was that they had fallen in love in the past and the person they loved left them for someone else. Fear and mistrust entered this person and they were afraid of getting hurt again so would not stay long in any relationship. If things became too intimate they would break the relationship. They were not willing to commit to anyone, trust had to be redeveloped in their life once they came to terms with the root of their problem, then they could form and develop a relationship in a healthy way.

People who have been hurt by others will hurt people in return unless they deal with their hurt. Pick a murderer, paedophile or sex offender and look into their history and you will often find that they were hurt themselves as children or even adults and because their hurt had not been dealt with, it developed into anger and rage which took over their lives. When anger has not been dealt with, it will lead to demonic oppression and eventually possession which leads to destruction.

This is a subject that I explore in detail in my book, 'Protecting Your Greatest Asset: Your Mind'.

Have you ever wondered how a 10 year old can rape, torture and murder another child? What has happened to the conscience? Uncontrolled anger will lead to a dead conscience; anger lies in the bosom of a fool.

When a person picks up offences easily they will be in danger, for anger if not checked will open all kinds of evil doors. This is why we need to walk in forgiveness, Jesus said forgive 77 by 77 times and pray, forgive us as we forgive others.

1 Corithians 10:13, *"There is no temptation which you have gone through which is not common to man: but God is faithful, who will not suffer you to be tempted above what you are able; but will with the temptation also make a way to escape, that you may be able to bear it."*

When you are faced with someone whose problem is fear, read through scriptures on fear and help them to understand the love of God and their security in Christ. Try to build their confidence in the scriptures. Let them realise that their fear is of something they imagine, something unknown, and the love of God will be like a bright light shining into the darkness, showing them a path to safety.

Phippians 4:6-7, *"Be anxious for nothing; but in every thing by prayer and supplication with thanksgiving let your requests be made known to God. And the peace of God, which passes all understanding, will keep your hearts and minds through Christ Jesus."*

Remember as a man thinks in his heart, so is he.

Discouragement and hopelessness

Before you can effectively help someone who suffers with depression, you need to first understand that depression is only a symptom of a deeper problem. Discouragement and hopelessness is usually the starting point of depression. The biggest cause of backsliding amongst believers is discouragement, yet what causes discouragement or hopelessness?

- When people face difficulties in life and they don't understand why or how they can overcome them

- When someone fails to achieve their set goals and they lack the patience to wait on God

- When we begin to envy those who we deem to be successful where we have failed

- When there is a delay in receiving an answer to our prayers.

These difficulties breed hopelessness and a defeated spirit and this in turn causes discouragement which, if not checked quickly, will produce depression and complete loss of faith. Discouragement destroys courage, confidence or hope. It stops someone from doing anything as they become gloomy and dejected.

The heart faints under a discouraged spirit and will need to be revived again.

The only way to combat discouragement is through hope, and hope comes through having a solid foundation in life.

Matthew 7:24-27, *"Therefore whoever hears these sayings of mine, and does them, I will liken him to a wise man, who built his house upon a rock.*

And the rain descended, and the floods came, and the winds blew, and beat upon that house; and it fell not: for it was founded upon a rock.

And every one that hears these sayings of mine, and does them not, shall be likened to a foolish man, who built his house upon the sand.

And the rain descended, and the floods came, and the winds blew, and beat upon that house; and it fell, and great was the fall of it."

Hope depends on what you know about the person you are trusting or the circumstances surrounding the situation. If I trust the person or I know without any shadow of doubt that there is a chance for them then I have hope. As a Christian, if I believe in Christ and his love and this foundation is heavily laid in my life then I have hope because I can trust in his unfailing love. David sums this up well in the Psalms.

Psalms 42:5, *"Why art thou cast down, O my soul? and why art thou disquieted in me? hope thou in God: for I shall yet praise him for the help of his countenance."*

To deal with discouragement, you need to understand God's purpose for human life. You must come to a place where you can trust that God knows what he is doing even when everything else suggests otherwise. You need to understand God's purpose for each individual life.

One day God took the prophet Jeremiah to the Potters house, and his story tells us more about understanding God's purpose through the trials of life.

Jeremiah 18:1-6, *"The word which came to Jeremiah from the LORD, saying, Arise, and go down to the potter's house, and there I will cause you to hear my words. Then I went down to the potter's house, and behold, he wrought a work on the wheels. And the vessel that he made of clay was marred in the hand of the potter: so he made it again another vessel, as it seemed good to the potter to make it. Then the word of the LORD came to me, saying, O house of Israel, cannot I do with you as this potter? says the LORD. Behold, as the clay is in the potter's hand, so are you in my hand, O house of Israel."*

There is a purpose for each of our lives, just like the potter makes different vessels for different purposes. Each vessel is shaped in a mould according to its future purpose. For example some cooking vessels will be put through a fiery furnace as they will need to stand a lot of heat through out their existence, again the amount of heat will depend on the purpose for which it will be used.

Yet still some vessels will go through the furnace seven times in order for them to become vessels of honour, shining and beautiful for noble use. Some vessels do not need all this as they just need to be left to dry such as the mud pots, these vessels are so fragile and break very easily and yet they have their purpose, if you use them in the heat they will be destroyed.

In human terms, the more the trials, the hotter the fire, then know that you are being prepared to be a vessel of honour.

1 Peter 1:16 -17, *"In which you greatly rejoice, though now for a season (if need be) you are in heaviness through manifold temptations: That the trial of your faith, being much more precious than of gold that perishes, though tried with fire, might be found to praise, and honour, and glory, at the appearing of Jesus Christ."*

Psalms 66:8 -12, *"O bless our God, ye people, and make the voice of his praise to be heard: Who holds our soul in life, and suffers not our feet to be moved. For you, O God, have proved us: you have tried us, as silver is tried. You have brought us into the net; you have laid affliction upon our loins. You have caused men to ride over our heads; we went through fire and through water: but you brought us out into a wealthy place."*

One needs to see the spiritual work being performed in our lives through the circumstances which we are going through. Only then can you truly understand why scripture says that all these things work together for your good, meaning that the things which happen to you which seem good and bad together work to shape and guide you within God's purpose.

Scripture tells us to consider it a blessing when we go through these trials for great will be our reward if we faint not. The finished product is truly the pride of its maker and everyone will desire it.

However, not all circumstances in our lives are the result of God working in us. You need to first check if you are suffering due to your own wrong doing, as you may actually be reaping the fruit of your own rebellious ways and should be repenting rather than deceiving yourself. It is so easy to apply the word of God wrongly and end up in deception.

Surely he is God in the valley, God on the mountain top, God in the morning and God in the night time.

Psalms 113:3, *"From the rising of the sun to the going down of the same the LORD'S name is to be praised."*

The Counselling Session

The first few words spoken by the individual are very significant. The Bible says that out of the abundance of the heart the mouth speaks. Equally at the end of the session, the last words will give you an indication as to whether the session was helpful or not.

Always watch out for repeated references to a situation or denial that there is a problem as these may give you clues that this is an area of concern or what the real issues are. Always be sensitive to concealed meanings in the individual's body language or the way they phrase their words. Sometimes a person may start to say something and then suddenly change to talk about something else or completely avoid answering a question, this shows that there is something they are not comfortable with so don't let the opportunity to probe pass by.

Be careful however that you do not probe too deep too quickly. The timing is very important, you can note something and get back to it in your next session by simply saying, "Would you like to explore further what you mentioned last time?"

A counselling session must have a structure; from the beginning let the person know what time the session will end or how long the session will take. Be a good time keeper, whatever you do don't go on and on and remember it's not about you but the person you are counselling. Setting a time limit lets them know that time is precious and they are not there to indulge their problem but to find a solution for it.

Your body posture is very important; smile to give assurance and avoid putting answers in a person's mouth. Let them reflect and come up with their own answers. Allow periods of silence in between as the person might be reflecting, but don't let the gap be too wide to create uneasiness.

Traditional Christian counselling sometimes tends to instruct the individual on what actions to take, but this can lead to control and reliance rather than helping someone to come up with their own solutions. Traditional Christian counselling has tended to produce dependency rather than spiritual growth and accountability for one's actions, thus the repetition of problems as lessons are not learnt.

Some questions may sound very accusatory and one's tone of voice can reveal unspoken suspicions which can arouse fear and antagonism. In the beginning, I said that a counsellor is a facilitator, therefore one must possess skills which will help in exploring, understanding, evaluating and putting together an action plan. The reason why much counselling in the church is ineffective is because there is no professionalism accompanying counselling. Usually it becomes an informal chat which can be unproductive if it only gives the person the opportunity to offload their problems and not take responsibility for solving them. Effective counselling must set goals and have outcomes, even if those outcomes are viewed as negative.

Stages of Counselling

Relationship

Aim to establish a good relationship, explore thoughts, feelings and behaviour. Allow the person to feel the emotion inside them and to recognise what that emotion is so that they can deal with it squarely. If the person breaks down don't tell them to stop. Offer a tissue, perhaps a glass of water and allow them to let that emotion out.

Recognition

Help the person to recognise the pieces of the puzzle and to piece them together in order to see the full picture. Usually themes and patterns will emerge that need to be pointed out in order to gain an understanding and to identify strengths and weaknesses. Where there is a need for confrontation, do it so as not to offend.

Remember, you are dealing with adults who need to be respected and loved regardless of their failings or problems. Remember that belief systems sometimes need to be challenged in order to move forward.

Identify solutions

Help the individual to identify ways of solving their problem. Set goals, support and see that the person is in agreement with all the decisions made. Remember that you can not dictate, you are a facilitator. Otherwise, the experience will not lead to the desired effect.

Action plan

Have an action plan and set a time limit, then review the plan and see how the person's life and situation have changed. Depending on the maturity and willingness of the person and the complexity of their situation, you may need a few sessions.

This is what the Bible calls discipleship, as Jesus worked in a similar way with his disciples. Jesus challenged their lack of faith, asking them, "Who do men say I am?", then he asked, "Who do you think I am?"

In other words, challenge their thinking on the subject, personalise the issue and put them in a position where they are forced to take a deeper look at their belief system and then make a choice to change, if that is what they want.

Jesus sent his disciples out to perform tasks and when they came back, they gave him feedback. He praised them when they did well, corrected them when they were wrong.

Family dynamics

As a counsellor you need to understand family dynamics. People are a product of their environmental, cultural and spiritual beliefs. Their upbringing plays a major role in how they perceive things. Never assume you know how the person thinks just from the way that they look.

Although people may come from the same background, each family will have its own way of functioning. It is important therefore to understand the different types of family situations such as; lone parent families, step families, half Christian families and non Christian families.

Each family will differ in their values and relationships and each family must be taken as an individual case.

There are a lot of things that happen within families which are sometimes kept as a family secret. Usually when abuse takes place within the family it is an embarrassing thing so it is swept under the carpet, but the abused individual receives no support to deal with their pain, anger and sense of betrayal.

You may come across such situations where this might be the root of someone's problems which could manifest as health, spiritual, emotional or physical problems.

Usually, the person will be feeling guilty about the incident and about exposing the family and how this would affect relationships at home. It is important that the individual can trust the counsellor completely; otherwise they will not open up.

One day, we were having a group discussion when the topic turned to relationships. One lady said that she was not on speaking terms with her brother; they had fallen out, the reason for which she did not reveal but she was certain that she could never forgive him.

Another lady added that she was not speaking to her father and was not prepared to forgive him either. One by one people began to relate their own experiences of unforgiveness and bitterness. What they all shared in common was that they did not enjoy good health.

I had to explain to them the connection between their bitterness and sickness, so I told the story of a man who was dying of cancer. I accompanied a relative of his to visit him in his home. This man was very upset, saying that he had missed Benny Hinn's meeting due to lack of transport, and he believed that if he had attended, he would have been healed. As I sat listening to him, the Holy Sprit said, "Tell him that even if he had attended the meeting he would not have been healed because of bitterness in his heart."

When I told him this, the man broke down and wept, and when he was composed again he said to me, "You do not know what my father and brother did to me, I can never forgive them".

It turned out that he had not seen or spoken to them for some years. I explained that because of all this bitterness he was feeding the cancer. The Bible tells us that when we pray, say, "forgive us as we forgive those who sin against us". If you do not forgive then you can not be forgiven.

Isaiah 59:1-2, *"Behold, the Lord's hand is not shortened, that it cannot save; neither his ear heavy that it cannot hear: But your iniquities have separated between you and your God, and your sins have hid his face from you, that he will not hear."*

This man explained that it was difficult to forgive as it had gone on for too many years, and I explained that he had a choice between forgiving them and be healed or not to forgive and die and go to hell. He chose to forgive and God healed him, the cancer disappeared.

On his own he could not forgive, but with God, all things are possible. Forgiveness is a choice, your mind will submit to whatever thoughts you feed it with. You can choose to be angry, pick up offences or to walk in love and tell yourself it does not matter. You can reassure yourself that it's really not important, its only your pride which is wounded but life must go on.

Bitterness will destroy your life, it will rob you of happiness and freedom and your life will never be the same. Don't spend your life bitter, frustrated and angry, it's not worth it.

The man invited his father and brother and the many years of silence were broken and the family was healed.

One thing to remember is that you are also still open to learning new things and as you counsel others, you might begin to learn about yourself as well. Be open to the spirit and repent of those areas in your own life that might be highlighted by other people's problems.

The word of God is a double edged sword or even a mirror, so while you try and make others see their image, through it your image will also be visible. It is always good to be reflective and to search your own heart lest you be a sign post for others while you yourself are disqualified.

Be a vessel of honour, fit for the master's use. Whatever you do, let the love of God flow through you to others. Be sensitive to the Holy Spirit who is our comforter and counsellor; allow him to counsel through you.

BEING COUNSELLED

What if you are the one needing guidance or counselling?

First of all, if you need counselling you need to find out more about the person who is going to counsel you. Is this person a mature Christian? Do they have a good reputation in the church? Is this person under submission, trained and known by church leaders to be counselling people? What is in it for them? Is this a job or a ministry? Do they come highly recommended or are they just a friend?

Next, you need to look at what are you hoping to gain from the counselling. What are your expectations? Are you looking for an opportunity to just offload your problems or do you want real tangible outcomes and actions? How much are you willing to open yourself to the counsellor? Are you prepared to be challenged in the way you think or see things?

If you take a University degree in counselling, part of the certification process requires you to receive counselling yourself. This is not because there is anything 'wrong' with you, it is because it is very valuable for you to personally experience the counselling relationship from both sides.

It is a good idea for you to approach someone for counselling, and to choose that person based on them being different to you, with different experiences and different opinions so that they can truly challenge you and help you to explore your beliefs and practices.

Remember that a counsellor is there to facilitate and to guide you through the scriptures so you can make informed choices. At the end of the day you and you alone should make the final decision. A good counsellor knows they can not force or manipulate you into submitting to their opinions or advice.

If your counsellor starts to force you to do anything that violates your conscience then you should not continue with the counselling sessions. Never submit yourself to be hypnotised in any way, as that is surrendering your will and your mind to another person and this is very dangerous. Some counsellors would like to just tell you what you should do and not give you the right to make that choice, and this too is wrong. A good counsellor will help you to explore the issue and arrive at your own conclusions and decisions.

Even if you disagree with the method of counselling, don't just reject it, learn from it.

Jesus, who is the mighty counsellor, did not force his opinion on any man. While at supper, he reveals that one of the disciples would betray him. He knew it would be Judas as the scriptures say, yet Jesus did not say, "Judas, why do you choose to do this evil? Repent now or else you will go to hell". Judas knew the word and had every opportunity to do what was right, yet instead Jesus said, "Go and do what you must do", in other words, you have a choice but since you choose to do wrong when you know what is right then its your choice and you will have to bear the consequences.

You have a choice at the end of the counselling session to do what you have been advised or to do the opposite. If you don't feel comfortable about the guidance you have received then you have a right to seek a second opinion before putting the advice into practice. If you ever feel uncomfortable about the way the sessions are conducted then you should never ignore your conscience because that's another way that God speaks to you to warn you about things which may be likely to go wrong, so follow your conscience and trust in God's way.

It is important to note that all the wisdom in the world will not help the person unless God is part of the solution. This is why the psychologist and all hypnotists have not had a good record of success, the problem most of the time comes back.

Alcohol Anonymous have been helping people for so many years, yet look at how many times celebrities are back in rehab. Without the Holy Spirit we can not bring lasting change in people's lives. This is why, as a Christian counsellor, you need to depend on the guidance of the Holy Spirit at all times.

God alone can transform peoples' lives.

Counselling and the Deliverance Ministry

There are times when you are counselling someone and you sense that their problem has a demonic root. Not every problem has to do with demons; some people have become so deeply involved with the so called deliverance ministry that they see demons in everything and in everyone. People have endured untold sufferings at the hands of bogus pastors and prophets who use their own beliefs, traditions and fears to trap them. It is unfortunate that some people have had bad experiences from the so called deliverance ministries, but that does not negate the fact that demons are there and they do possess people and people do need to be delivered from demonic oppression and possession. The Bible is very clear on these matters

Whenever you visit a church or a so called man of God, if they start by talking witchcraft, leave immediately. Jesus never preached witchcraft, he commanded demons out and healed the sick, yet never once did he accuse anyone of witchcraft or tell anyone they had been bewitched. If you have the power of God then just minister deliverance to the captives, they don't need to know where the disease came from; they just want to be well. If you are asked to pay for healing or deliverance then this is not of God so leave or you may as well visit a witchdoctor or fortune teller or spirit medium because they will tell you the same things.

The gifts of God are not for sale, and the power of God is given freely so the people of God can benefit. Be warned, we are in the end times where people are greedy for gain and pastors have become hired hands. No doubt they will have their reward.

There are, however, genuine cases were someone's problems or sickness may have a demonic origin. There are many examples in the Bible in the ministry of Jesus.

One day a lady visited us requiring some counselling, saying that she was having problems with people generally and that for some reason people just disliked her. She began to seek help when this started to affect her work as she was a school teacher. The students and other teachers did not get on with her and she found herself becoming more and more isolated.

We were trying to find out when these events started and what was happening around her during that period before we decided to pray and ask God to guide us. When we began to pray this lady began to manifest, my husband came to help me cast out the demons from her. The demon began to speak saying, "we are not going anywhere" we asked why and the demon said "Because we were killed by John (not the real name) who made spells to make his business flourish, he gave us this place for us to live in so we are not going anywhere".

We told the demons to shut up and then talked to the woman and asked her to confess her sins, invite Jesus into her life and confess Jesus as Lord of her life. The woman did all that we asked her to do and we then started to cast out the demons again, but again they were saying, "No, we have a right to be here, you can't chase us", so we said, "You have just lost your right as this woman has given her life to Jesus, Jesus now has a right and he commands you to come out of her and go to the dry places where you belong."

The demons screamed and said, "OK we are going but allow us to pass at her house and collect some of our things from under her bed and also in her classroom in school." The demon came out of her and she fell to the floor as if lifeless. After a time, she got up and sat down, and we asked who John was. She said, "He is my father". We asked if she had known the other two people mentioned by the demons and she said, "Yes, those people died mysteriously just around the time I started experiencing these problems". A week later, this woman called to tell us her father was very angry at what she had done in getting rid of the spirits. Her father was pleading with her to go back with him so that they could fix things. We warned this woman that if she went back with her father, he would put the spirits back and her condition would be seven times worse, just as the Bible says.

Witchcraft is very much alive and it doesn't matter whether you are European, African or Asian, as witchcraft knows no boundaries, race, or colour of skin, it exists in a different form in all these communities. It is of utmost importance that as a minister you understand that our job is not to chase after demons or witches. In the ministry of Jesus, we see that he concentrated on healing people, not on where, how or who put the evil spirit or disease in the person. Witch hunting is not biblical at all, and as a minister you should operate in love, not in judgement of people.

The devil is the accuser of the brethren, so don't be his partner.

The problem we see today is that anyone can open their own ministry without having served under someone else to receive mentoring. Due to ignorance, some so-called pastors are using familiar spirits and therefore accuse everyone of witchcraft or demon possession. It is clear that the motivation of some people is greed and financial gain rather than love for people and the work of God, thus Jesus said they shall say on the day of Judgement, "did we not heal the sick and cast out demons in your name?" and he will say to them, "depart from me you workers of iniquity, I never knew you". These men or women charge for their services when the Bible clearly teaches that freely you received the gift from God so freely give it for others to benefit from.

Jesus taught us that, in a big house, there are vessels, some to honour and some to dishonour, and he also taught a parable about a farmer. The farmer planted good crops in his field but when his servants went to see, they were surprised that there were a lot of weeds. They requested to uproot all the weeds but were told "let it grow together, else in trying to uproot the weeds you uproot good crops as well; at harvest time however the weeds will be separated and burnt". Again, Jesus said that there are many who say "Lord, Lord" who shall not enter the Kingdom of God so don't be fooled, evil doers shall have their reward. Do not be a casualty of your own ignorance or someone else's ignorance or greed.

As I have said, there is genuine deliverance which sets people free from bondage without labelling them and it comes free of charge because Jesus has already paid the price. If you are ever asked to pay for your healing or deliverance then know that you are in dangerous hands and you should get out of the situation as quickly as you can.

Most of what is called schizophrenia, people hearing voices or having a split personality is of demonic origin. People who take drugs open themselves to all kinds of evil spirits who are looking for a house to live in. Demons look for people who they can possess so that they can use a body to do their filthy work.

If someone is possessed, they are not evil, it is not the person but the spirit using the person that you deal with. The person must be treated with respect and dignity; Jesus always treated people with dignity, love and compassion. People were never a means to an end and I sometimes wonder what Jesus would say about some of the goings on in the church today. There is no more difference between the church of Jesus Christ and cults who use familiar spirits and engage in witchcraft although they see witchcraft in other people.

Jeremiah 23:11, *"For both prophet and priest are profane; even in my house have I found their wickedness, says the LORD."*

Jeremiah 23:13, *"And I have seen folly in the prophets of Samaria; they prophesied in Baal, and caused my people Israel to err."*

Jeremiah 23:14, *"I have seen also in the prophets of Jerusalem a horrible thing: they commit adultery, and walk in lies: they strengthen also the hands of evil-doers, that none doth return from his wickedness: they are all of them to me as Sodom, and the inhabitants of it as Gomorrah."*

God will judge all evil doers, it does not matter how they deceive themselves and others who are like minded. God will not be mocked, and whatever a man sows he shall reap.

Demons can enter your body when you are under the influence of drugs or alcohol, or when you allow someone to hypnotize you. You are at risk when you are not in full control of yourself. The demons find a way into your life. When people are grieving, they are also very vulnerable, and when you allow anger to go unchecked it will open a door. This is why the Bible says that it is not wrong to be angry but don't let the sun go down while you are still angry.

Understanding the spiritual realm is very important, you need to know about the ministry of angels and the ministry of demons. This is why I have said from the beginning that counselling should be undertaken by mature, well trained people as you may have to deal with spiritual problems as well.

The world today would like to believe that there are no evil spirits, and this is a mistake. However, some people have also taken a truth and manipulated it to suit their own purposes. This only adds to confusion and causes people to reject the truth as they are no longer sure of what is going on.

The Bible tells the story of a man who lived in the graveyard until he met with Jesus. His name was Legion, and the demons within him said "there are many of us". Jesus commanded the demons to come out of him, they requested to go into a herd of pigs which, when possessed, jumped into the sea and drowned.

What about spirits of divination? Paul cast out such a spirit from a young girl who had followed them for days, prophesying "these men are the servants of the living God, listen to them". This spirit was posing as a spirit of prophecy from God so as to deceive people. Paul saw through this spirit and cast it out in Jesus' name. The problem today is that there are few people who can discern the spirits, thus the confusion. The false spirits parading as prophets of God have caused so much destruction and hurt so many people in the process.

I preached at a church in Botswana some years ago, and the Spirit of the Lord was present to heal. After the meeting, a young lady came to me and gave her testimony. This lady said that she was struggling as she felt that she could not cope with living with a man, she felt as if they were two men living together. Her husband also sensed that something was wrong and the relationship was strained. She said that during the worship something came out of her and she was left feeling so very different.

This girl said to me that when she was born her parents were very disappointed as they had been expecting a boy. They had prepared everything for a boy and so she wore boy's clothes from birth. As a teenager, she was known as a "Tomboy" because she never wore dresses like other girls. She said that she had always felt like a boy in a girl's body.

This woman confessed that she actually felt something come out of her body, she also said that for the first time she felt different and this was very strange to her. I explained that due to that strong desire by her parents to have a son and their rejection of her as a girl, they opened a door for the male spirit which entered her as a child. She felt like a boy and for all those years while growing up she was a boy in a girl's body but could not talk to anyone for fear of being made an outcast. Now that the spirit had left her, she was free to continue and enjoy her marriage. I know this may be hard to believe for some people but these things are very true in as much as they are difficult to explain.

You see, her problems were not that she was not a good wife but rather of demonic background. No amount of counselling would solve this kind of problem and the person will not volunteer this information as it is a very sensitive issue which is frowned upon by the church. People always assume that homosexuality is a chosen lifestyle; I believe this not to be true in every case such as this one. With most people, it is something which is in them from birth, and spirits may have entered whilst still in the womb or during the childhood stage. For some, yes it is a chosen lifestyle and that is why they can be bisexual at times.

The world today refuses to believe that there are evil spirits around that will enter your life and begin to live through your body while you are held captive. But this is why Jesus came to open prison doors and to set the captives free.

Luke 4:18-19, *"The spirit of the Lord is upon me, because he has anointed me to preach the gospel to the poor; he has sent me to heal the broken-hearted, to preach deliverance to the captives, and recovering of sight to the blind, to set at liberty them that are bruised, To preach the acceptable year of the Lord."*

Conclusion

Counselling is a very important part of pastoral care and body ministry. It is the only other tool apart from preaching and teaching which can ensure a healthy flock that will grow and come to maturity as God intended. The church is a spiritual hospital and there should be qualified workers in order to avoid casualties.

As we have seen, a church can also be a place where people can be wounded, damaged and destroyed in the hands of immature, untrained workers, false teachers and prophets.

Jeremiah 23:1-4, *"Woe be to the pastors that destroy and scatter the sheep of my pasture! says the LORD. Therefore thus says the LORD God of Israel against the pastors that feed my people; Ye have scattered my flock, and driven them away, and have not visited them: behold, I will visit upon you the evil of your doings, says the LORD. And I will gather the remnant of my flock from all countries whither I have driven them, and will bring them again to their folds; and they shall be fruitful and increase. And I will set shepherds over them who shall feed them: and they shall fear no more, nor be dismayed, neither shall they be lacking, says the LORD."*

The Holy Spirit is the spirit of counsel; he is looking for vessels he can use to give guidance and direction to his flock. God never intended that ministers control and manipulate the people, but rather that they use scripture to guide, correct and discipline.

Isaiah 42:16, *"And I will bring the blind by a way that they knew not; I will lead them in paths that they have not known: I will make darkness light before them, and crooked things straight. These things will I do for them, and not forsake them."*

Isaiah 30:21, *"And thy ears shall hear a word behind thee, saying, This is the way, walk ye in it, when ye turn to the right hand, and when ye turn to the left."*

Counselling is seeking direction and guidance in everyday life issues which may threaten our peace and harmony firstly with God, then with others and indeed within oneself. God desires to lead and guide his people throughout their journey here on Earth.

This is why Jesus promised the disciples that he would never leave nor forsake them, Jesus said, "I will be with you until the end". You are never alone in your situation. Allow God to take you by the hand and lead you in the way that he has prepared for you.

Proverbs 15:22, *"Without counsel purposes are disappointed: but in the multitude of 'Godly' counsellors they are established."*

Psalms 48:14, *"For this God is our God for ever and ever: he will be our guide even unto death."*

Don't be too quick to act, wait on the Holy Spirit and he will give you revelation and wisdom in how to deal with many difficult situations.

Remember, anything done without love is not of God, regardless of who is doing it.

Amen!

Protecting Your Greatest Asset: Your Mind

Merica Cox's first book explored the steps that we can take to ensure our mental well being, following the principles of spiritual guidance.

The Lord has not left us at the mercy of Satan and his demons; he is raising us into an army that will destroy Satan's prisons and let the captives go free. We are not fighting alone. Jesus fights alongside us.

The battle for the mind is still going on today. Satan uses everything he can to try to confuse, weaken and eventually destroy our minds.

Don't give him your mind - stand up and fight.

"Our greatest struggles are in the mind and this book attempts to give its readers a better understanding of the mind and how we could handle this war. This book is a must read!"

Pastor Ivan Moodley

Protecting Your Greatest Asset: Your Mind
Merica Cox
CGW Publishing
2009
ISBN 978-0-9565358-1-8

THE BALM OF GILEAD WORLD MINISTRIES

Balm of Gilead World Ministries was started in 1996 by Merica and Joel Cox in Bulawayo, Zimbabwe for the Glory of God.

The family had returned to Zimbabwe from Zambia where they had served as missionaries and the church began in their family home in North End. The first service was attended by 15 people and three months later the meetings moved to a college hall in Lobengula Street. The church continued to grow and six months later the meetings moved again to the bigger hall at the Academy of Music.

The name Balm of Gilead comes from Jeremiah chapter 8 verse 22, "Is there no Balm in Gilead, is there no physician there? Why then is not the health of the daughter of my people recovered?

The Balm of Gilead logo came to Merica in a vision which she saw a rainbow, inscribed with the words "What is your hearts desire?". She answered, "To be like Jesus and to do the works which Jesus did, even greater works" and then saw a cloud ascending and lifting the rainbow higher into the sky. Merica chose the rainbow as a reminder of what she felt was a covenant with God, just as God made a covenant with Noah and gave him a rainbow for a sign.

In 2001, Merica came to the United Kingdom and settled in High Wycombe, starting a church in her lounge in Dashwood Avenue. The group later moved to Green Street Community Centre, again to the Reggie Grove Centre and later to the current location at the Wye Valley Community Centre.

In 2005, due to the number of people who were commuting from east London, another branch was opened in Romford, Essex.

In 2006 the Cox family moved to Wellingborough in Northamptonshire where a few months later they started holding services, giving birth to yet another branch.

We thank the Lord for his faithfulness and pray he will use this ministry as a tool in His Hand for His Glory.

You can learn more about the Balm of Gilead World Ministries at our website:

www.bogministries.org

info@bogministries.org

www.ingramcontent.com/pod-product-compliance
Lightning Source LLC
Chambersburg PA
CBHW071720040426
42446CB00011B/2153